Few people are in motion as much and as often as American Indians. Travel is, of course, more than recreation or even a way of life for American Indian people. Journeys were and remain a way of staying in touch with our first mother, the Earth. They're a result of seeing home as not just a place surrounded by human-made walls, but anywhere we find ourselves between Earth and Sky.

Some of the finest contemporary poems written by Indian authors deals with travel. They range from sacred journeys and pilgrimages on the one hand to tragic tales of displacement on the other—Trails of Tears and Long Walks that ancestors survived and their descendants will never forget. Such writers as Simon Ortiz and Joy Harjo and Luci Tapahonso have put together wonderful collections like that which both reflect such journeys and take the reader with them. I've always been delighted by their multi-layered volumes of poetry. And now I have another such book to love.

Lee Francis's ON THE GOOD RED INTERSTATE is firmly within the tradition of American Indian "tribal travel poetry." It both instructs and delights the reader as you are transported in more ways than one. There is an abundant store of both laughter and tears, gritty reality and gentle vision here. It passes effortlessly back and forth between past and present, between east and west, and between the worlds of the author's ancestors—Indian and non-Indian alike, finding that place between Laguna and Lebanon where bloods flow together and dreams grow strong. Hitch a ride with Lee Francis—you might end up just about anywhere, but you'll be glad you took the journey.

Joe Bruchac

On the Good Red Interstate

*Truck Stop Tellings
and Other Poems*

Lee Francis

published by Taurean Horn Press
P.O. Box 641097
San Francisco, CA 94164-1097
ISBN 0-931552-12-5
Printed in the United States of America

Table of Contents

CHANGING SONGS

BLUE MOUNTAIN SONGS

Introduction

Many who know me are well aware of an obsession of mine: truck stops. Long before there were chain-restaurants like Denny's and Mickey D's (MacDonalds), there were truck stops. Growing up out in the country I became a frequent customer at Chief's Rancho, an early wanna-be truck stop west of Cubero, New Mexico. Hard, old-time, country music would blare from the radio or from the jukebox that required a quarter for five songs. I would usually sit at the counter acting all grown-up at age twelve while trying to drink the thick sheep-camp coffee from a chipped white porcelain mug.

I would pretend I was "on the road" traveling to somewhere like California. I wasn't too clear about what was beyond Albuquerque some sixty miles east, so I would sometimes pretend that I was going to Oklahoma City or "St. Louie." I knew about those two cities because of the song about driving from St. Louis to San Bernardino on US Route 66. It would be another decade before the Interstate Highway System would enable people to drive at 60 to 70 miles per hour on four-lane highways from the East Coast to the West Coast. In my vain attempt at acting grown-up, I would listen to the other travelers, mostly truck drivers, talking. Their stories fascinated me.

Parenthetically I would add that today, much has changed. Only a few of the "old time" truck stops remain. Now there are chain Truck Stop Travel Plazas. I was recently permanently banned from the Flying J Travel Plaza in Albuquerque by Jolene, the General Manager, because I was there "all the time" (according to Jim Baker, Vice President for Interstate Operations at the Flying J Corporate offices in Ogden, Utah). Such behavior as "being there all the time" is forbidden by Flying J. Maybe I was banned because I am Laguna Pueblo and we now have our own Travel Plaza and Casino. Banning me is Flying J's way of dealing with competition. I look forward to many newspaper articles with the headline: *Native American Poet and Storyteller banned from Flying J Travel Plaza*. T/A, Rip Griffins, Dancing Eagle Casino and Travel Plaza, and Petro don't have any problem with my being there all the time, listening to the wonderful stories told by the drivers.

Every summer, when I was a child, my parents would load all of us (my siblings and me) into the car and we would usually drive to California. We would leave Cubero at some ungodly hour like 3:00AM. The backseat was crammed full with children and we drove, for what seemed to a small child like two centuries, to Flagstaff, Arizona on US Route 66. As I remember, we usually arrived around noon. My dad would pull off the highway (there were no rest areas like there are today) and stop at a place shaded by tall pine trees. We all piled out of the car and mom would get out the food, which always included fried chicken, for our roadside picnic. To this day, whenever I eat cold fried chicken, I have a flashback of those long-ago picnics.

After we ate our hurried lunch, we climbed back into the car and continued on our drive. We usually managed to get to Kingman, Arizona around 4:00 PM and check into the Flamingo Motel. I loved that motel. It had a swimming pool and in those days when car air conditioning was uncertain, we were all ready for an hour in the water before going to eat dinner. We went to a restaurant that served mostly Chinese food. Children could choose to have a hot dog or hamburger. Regardless of what we decided to eat (which was most often a hamburger), my mother insisted that we eat some of the Chinese food she had ordered. "At least try it," she would command. At an early age I developed a "taste" for a variety of "ethnic" foods, other than Mexican, which were not usually pre-pared in New Mexico in the 1950s.

It was sheer agony to wait for an hour after eating dinner before being allowed to get back in the motel swimming pool. Neither of my parents could swim so they were hyper-careful to require that all of the kids stay in the shallow end of the pool. It was not until we were able to demonstrate we could "swim" unassisted that we were allowed to go into the deep (five feet) end. By 9:00PM, the sun had set and we were hustled off to bed. The second part of the journey from Kingman to Newport Beach in California was always arduous.

Around 4:00AM, we got into the car. We were silent. Grumpy. Tired. Sleepy. Mom and dad only spoke when absolutely necessary. Half-asleep, I remember waking up from time to time feeling nauseous from motion sickness as we drove on the road which curved around and around down the mountain to Prescott, Arizona. After a couple of hours, the sun began to rise. We had crossed the Mojave Desert in the pre-dawn hours and had finally arrived in Barstow, California. The salt-sea air that mixed with orange from the unending fields of orange groves was overwhelm-ing. We would stop and eat breakfast in Barstow and then on to Victorville, San Bernardino and the beach towns of Long Beach, Huntington and, at long last, Newport.

We would arrive in the late afternoon and after changing into our beach clothes, we would make a mad dash to the ocean a hundred or so yards from the beach house owned by my Aunt Edith and Uncle Bob Gunn.[1]

Little did I know that the long jaunts by car during the summer with my parents and siblings were to be a forerunner of the many journeys I would make throughout my adult life. Some would say that it is only natural I would travel as much as I have since I am descended from a long line of travelers on both my father's and mother's side of the family.

My father's grandfather, Elias, traveled by boat from Rume (which is near Beirut), Lebanon to the United States in the 1800s. He was one of the many thousands who came to Ellis Island where he was given a new last name of Francis. The story I remember about Elias was that he traveled from the East Coast to the West Coast selling rosaries and holy water which he claimed had been blessed by the Pope. When he traveled through what was then the New Mexico territory, he decided that he liked the Spanish land grant town of Seboyeta. At that time, the town was said to be a major junction for travelers going north or south or east or west. He traveled back to Lebanon and brought back his wife and young son, Narciso, and settled in Seboyeta. But Seboyeta soon became a ghost town when the rudimentary single-lane road called US Route 66 was paved. I remember stories about my grandfather, Narciso, traveling to California, Colorado and Mexico when he was young.

My dad was always traveling. I remember I was about five or six when my dad told my mom, while we were eating breakfast, that he was going to New York and Philadelphia. I had heard about those places. I knew they were very, very far away. I remember, after my dad had gone, telling my mother that I was sad because I wouldn't get to see dad for a long time. For a six-year old, a long time is equivalent to eternity. My mother looked down at me with a puzzled frown. "What are you talking about? Your father will be home for dinner tonight." I was convinced that my father had a magic carpet (he was Lebanese after all) that would get him to and from New York in the blink of an eye. It wasn't until I was about eight or nine when I learned that the New York and Philadelphia where my dad traveled to were small family villages located about three miles from Cubero on the Laguna Pueblo reservation.

Dad and Mom always went away during the month of January. Just the two of them. It was their time to be with each other my mother would explain to me. When they returned, there were all kinds of presents for the kids, which they had brought from the magical cities they had visited.

When my dad was elected as Lieutenant Governor of New

Mexico, the traveling throughout the state of New Mexico was mind-boggling. I accompanied my parents on a majority of those trips as well as to the National Conferences of Lieutenant Governors held throughout the United States.

On my mother's side, her great-grandfather had come to the United States from Scotland prior to the War of 1812 and settled in Ohio. Her grandmother, Meta, also had traveled, perhaps most reluctantly, to Carlisle Indian School in Pennsylvania during the heyday of the Indian Boarding School experiment. She returned to Laguna, but her youngest sister, Seichu, remained in Pennsylvania.

My grandmother, Agnes, traveled with her second husband, Sidney (my step-grandfather), all over North America, including Canada and Mexico. After my granddad passed on, she took two long trips around the world. In addition to the presents, she brought back wonderful stories about every place she had visited.

And while I listened avidly to the stories told by my family about their travels when I was a young boy, it wasn't until I was sixteen that I actually thought about taking a journey on my own. I remember that I was sitting on the overstuffed couch in my grandmother's living room. It was late afternoon and I was talking with her about driving to California in a "gee-it-would-be-nice-but-I'm-too-scared" tone of voice. To this day, I can see her face frozen in a stiff mask that only Laguna women can make. After a minute or so of silence, I asked her what she thought. In a voice that would brook no opposition, she said: "Go! Go and travel and see the world while you're young." I doubt that she thought I would go and travel as much as I have over the past four decades.

Truth is, I know very few Laguna people who have not traveled extensively across the United States, Canada, Mexico and even Europe. When I was in my early twenties, I used to think I was one of the few who had traveled back and forth to California. Then I learned about the Laguna Colony in Richmond (northern California), as well as the Laguna Colonies of San Bernardino and Barstow.

When I was nineteen, I moved to San Francisco where I lived for a year. I returned to my home place and stayed there until I was ready to venture out again. I got a job with Trans World Airlines and, using my passes, visited most of the major cities of the United States and many in Europe.

After I was married, we lived in several towns and cities in northern and southern California. We also lived in Washington, DC and Fairfax, Virginia. In New Mexico, we have lived in Cubero, Laguna, Santa Fe, Panderies, and, of course, Albuquerque. My spouse would say that over the years instead of taking a vacation like other people, we moved.

I continue to travel to places throughout Indian Country for conferences and workshops as National Director of Wordcraft Circle of Native Writers and Storytellers, an international organization of Native and non-Native members.

When I went to Japan for a speaking engagement, Mary, my spouse, was again ready to pack her bags and move to Ryukyu (Okinawa). It was while I was in Ryukyu (Okinawa) that I was inspired to write the poem, Ohio Gozaiemas. Having followed the ancient Ruykyu poetic form of four syllables plus four syllables per line with four lines per stanza, I was told by the Master Poet (called a National Treasure in Japan) that I had mastered the form. The proof, he said, was in translating my words into the Ryukyuan language. Both he and his wife took my poem and rapidly translated it into Ryukyu. Then they chanted it to me, which is how the poetic form is given. I was overwhelmed. Several months after I returned from Japan, I suffered congestive heart failure and that ended any thoughts about moving so far from my home place of Laguna. However, because of the poem, the land and the memories of that experience are still fresh in my heart and mind.

Forty years after my first truck stop experiences, the Grand-mothers (Creator/Spirit) rained down blessings and I was inspired to write. I began the journey from where the sun first touches the land on the East Coast and ended on July 26th, St. Ann's Day, at my home place of Laguna Pueblo, New Mexico. As I traveled, I stopped at every truck stop. I listened and observed. Hastily, and as surrepti-tiously as possible, I wrote down what I heard and saw. I jotted notes about what I smelled and tasted and touched.

Perhaps some of the more important behaviors esteemed by Native people all across Turtle Island are listening and observing without intruding. *Journey Songs*, the first section of this collection of poetry, reflects my obsession with listening and observing. The "found" poems which incorporate the words of people at the truck stop—including drivers, hitchhikers, food servers and cashiers—are intermixed with "memory" and other poetic forms.

When the journey began, I vaguely experienced something, which I can only describe as being magnetically pulled to my home place. Sometimes it felt like the throbbing beat of a powwow drum. At other times it was as if every cell in my body was chanting, return to the home place, return to the home place, over and over again. When that feeling or experience was especially strong, I incorporated it into the poem.

I am convinced the inspiration for the second section of this collection was a gift because of the actual day when my journey ended at Laguna. For me, July 26th, St. Ann's Day, is significant because it is my mother's birthday. On that day, I was at Laguna and my thoughts were focused on my mother (who had passed on to the other side some years previously) and the women in my life who had cared for me, kept me centered, and taught me how to be a human being. To not include the mothers in the collection was unthinkable.

The poems in *Nyah Songs*, the second section, which celebrate the women in my life, were written over the past decade. "Nyah" is the Laguna Pueblo word for mother. Particular "formal poetic forms" in terms of meter/beat were sometimes employed as a way of capturing an important aspect of that person. For example, in "Nyah Agnes," a poem for my grandmother, I adapted the poetic style common to Keats and Donne. The poem, "Nyah Alene," for my mother-in-law, is rhymed because of her intense liking of poetry that rhymes.

Changing Songs, the third section, are reflections about the many harsh realities I have experienced over the past forty years. And while most might be seen as angry poems, for me, all evoke tears of anguish. In keeping with Native traditional way, these poems are about the not-good reflections, which balance the good ones. This effort to "walk in harmony/balance" with all of creation, seen and unseen, is central to Native traditions.

Blue Mountain Songs is the fourth section. For the People, four is significant because it acknowledges the four sacred directions as well as the four interrelated aspects of spirit, mind, heart, and body. Blue Mountain, also known as Mt. Taylor, is the mountain sacred to Laguna Pueblo people. The poems in this section focus on the incredibly wonderful and tragic experiences in my life including the death of my father, who had Alzheimers, and my own brush with the other side when I had a coronary.

For me, the work follows a decidedly logical progression. When viewed as a total work, the collection is a representation of my life experience. It is about what I have learned, what I am learning now, and what I hope to learn in the future. Like a Laguna Pueblo origin story, the collection begins with a journey to the home place. At the home place, the mothers of the People are celebrated and honored. It is to them that I bring the gift of the story about my journey. The poems that follow are about the harsh realities of life and serve to balance the not-harsh experiences. The work concludes with poems about living and dying, the generations (past - my father; present - myself; future - my son) and ends with a poem which focuses on the dream-time.

And while I have traveled extensively throughout my life, I still return to my home place. Perhaps it's a re-creation of all the journeys my parents and grandparents made in their time. When they returned to the home place they brought gifts and stories about their travels. I remember when anyone returned from a journey, we would go visit my relatives at Laguna. My Aunt Jessie, grandma's oldest sister, would be there along with Bec (Rebecca), her daughter, and other family (both by blood and those of Oak clan). Everyone would listen to the stories about the journey.

My son continues what might be called the family tradition of traveling. Now in his early twenties, he has traveled with friends to Chicago, Minneapolis, Florida and Colorado and has gone alone to New York City. He plans to go to Europe and god herself knows where else. When he returns from his travels, he always brings the gift of story about his journeys. Recently, after returning from a journey, he announced: "Shhhh. It's a magical story. You have to go on the journey with me." I am certain that he, too, will have many wonderful "amventures"[2] throughout his life.

You are invited to travel on a journey with me.

Lee Francis
Albuquerque

1. Uncle Bob, Robert Bruce Gunn, was my grandmother's uncle. He had traveled with his three brothers, Elgin, Kenneth Colin Campbell, and John Malcolm from Ohio to Laguna. Two of the brothers, John M. and Kenneth, stayed in Laguna. Kenneth (Gunn Clan of Carthness and Sutherland in Scotland) married my great-grandmother, Meta Atsye (Oak clan of Laguna Pueblo). After he passed on, his brother John married Meta. Elgin went to the Dakotas and Robert went to California.

2. The word, "amventure," was used by my son when he was a small child learning to speak when he meant adventure.

Journey Songs

Prologue

Where morning sun first touches
        the land of the People
I start on a journey
        to the place of beginning

On the good red interstate
        made sacred by the People
I travel across ancient land
        carry earth and abalone
        sage and tobacco

Return to the homeplace
        on Grandmother Spider's web
Return to the homeplace
        to the People of the White Lake
Return to the homeplace
        with gifts and stories
Return to the homeplace

Ocean City Clam Bake

Ocean City, Maryland

Like clams they lie
on buff-colored sand
as foggy sun
casts its dim light
and the seagull
carefully inspects its turf
head flits left to right
and back.

From out of the foggy mist
the Baywatch stud
walkie-talkie in hand
nervously paces the beach
carefully inspects his turf
head bobs left to right
and back

The clams lie quiet
enveloped in mid-morning fog
taking no notice of
the Baywatch stud
or the seagull.

Pinball Podium

Maryland I-95 SB [1]   Exit 57
Sunday 19 July
Baltimore

The trucker's chapel is set up
brown veneer podium
scratched and worn
no longer able to endure any
beating with a bible
stands in front of the large screen tv
and the itinerant preacher
waits patiently for his flock.

The driver walks in and says
"This the tv lounge?"
Preacher nods and says "yep"
"When's the movie come on?"
Preacher doesn't answer
and the driver leaves
to the sounds from the pinball game
      steel ball hits the bell
          ding ding
          ding ding
a modern version of
ancient tribal drum.

Tropical Jungle Dawn

Pennsylvania I-70 WB Exit 12
Monday 20 July 6:00AM
Breezewood

I.
Just before dawn drizzle
brings scant respite from
heat and humidity
or the bad attitude
of the clerk at the Motel 2 and a half
masquerading as a Ramada Inn.

II.
The too large truck stop building
reeks from the smell of
ammonia and bleach
and in the basement driver's lounge
the large screen tv blares
to an empty room.

III.
The long procession of trucks on I-70
wends its way through the
milky fog heading west
as air conditioners battle valiantly
against the heat and humidity
and the nameless radio announcer proclaims
>   "It's 6 AM and it's going to be
>   a hot one today folks."

Shower Time

Ohio I-70 WB Exit 122
Monday 20 July
Columbus

Through half-closed eyes
the drivers watch cartoon super-heroes
leap and bound in the driver's lounge.

Gone is the loudspeaker
from the tv room
that informed the world
about the shower
ready for a new occupant.

    last year we taped cardboard over it
    an irritation to be dealt with
    in truck driver fashion
    next year we'll tape cardboard over
    the wide-screen tv.

The cashier in the restaurant says loudly
     "We don't take Japanese money
     ONLY AMERICAN!"
The old couple confer in Japanese
     hand the grey-blond cashier
      a traveler's check and leave

Drivers waiting to pay for their food
pretend not to notice.

Changeling

Indiana I-70 WB Exit 156
Tuesday 21 July   12:30PM
State line of Ohio and "Indian-A"

Fifty feet beyond
the imaginary line
between two states
the destruction sign
warns drivers and
other patrons to
"Watch Your Step."
> No one notices the
> law enforcement officer
> with his hand on his
> holstered gun.

Inside, the driver orders sweet tea
and talks about Cobra and Northstar
Flirts with Cathy and tells her
he's been stuck here since 11 last night.

Heat and humidity
drown the diners
and no one is in any hurry
to go anywhere
least of all the drivers.

The law enforcement officer
has quietly disappeared.
At the place where he was standing
only a small puddle remains.

Trucker's Lament

Illinois I-70 WB Exit 159
Tuesday 21 July and Wednesday 22 July
Effingham

I.

Eyes glued to the Cherry Master
video slot machines right next to
the Country Pride restaurant
and the driver in the tv lounge
snores
        oblivious to the heat and humidity outside
        oblivious to the irritation of the other drivers
            trying to listen to their favorite Rosanne episode.

The radio announcer says it is 104
and the heat index is 110
        perhaps it is because they laughed
        about the topless Thunderbird.

And John with Werner wears a t-shirt
which boldly proclaims EASYRIDER
his sea-blue eyes like old turquoise
dance with that special light when he
says he's Choctaw and Cherokee.
        Must be so
        'cause his jokes
        are pure Ind'n humor
        and he says he knows
        how to make arrowheads.

II.

The shirtless curly blond hair man
in construction worker orange shorts
bellows and swears he will kill his brother
and five waitresses order him to
stop yelling and calm down.
They ask stupid questions
until the cops arrive.
        "I want my brother arrested" he demands
        "He lives at Post Office Box 1640."
After the cops leave
with their reports in quadruplicate
he asks the driver
smoking a Marlboro gold
for a cigarette.
        "You can have the rest of the pack."
        says John with Werner
            Sure must be Ind'n
            keeps givin' everythin' away
            and the heat and humidity
            reign victorious

III.

The five clocks announce the time in
LA, Denver, Effingham, New York and London.
Knowing the current time in London
is very important to every driver
especially the Australian
who drives for J. B. Hunt.

Between bites of eggs and bacon
he tells about drivin' "cross the stay-ets"
in an Australian accent
with a Southern American drawl
        maybe he's from south Australia
says he even knew
an aboriginal
back home.

8

Dream House

Ilinois I-70 Exit 18
Wednesday 22 July Noon
Troy

As she waddles from her truck
the big bellied driver
flinches from the heat
oblivious to the tourists from Canada
staring at her from their car.

The smell of testosterone
oozes from the driver's
mental condom and
impregnates the air in the
lounge where the movie
of choice is ConAir.

In the restaurant the driver
announces that he bought
his truck but didn't pay the
highway tax. The other driver
has his own story.

> "Been drivin' forty years"
> says the white-haired driver.
> "Quit when the wife took ill.
> Just stay'd home and made
> a miniTURE dream house
> we'd always wanted
> since we was first married."

Pale blue eyes stare into
a past reality of his life
and I remember another time
when Cubero Trading was
the only reality I understood.

> "Built it in the kitchen
> on the kitchen table.
> And when I finished,

9

I took it into our bedroom and
oh my did she smile.
Put it on a special shelf I built
just so's she could see it."

The clatter from dishes
being cleared from tables
sounds like mice scurrying
between the walls
as the universe stops to listen.

"She had a little smile on her face
looking at that house
when she passed on
'bout a week later."

He takes a long drag
from the unfiltered Camel cigarette
and smoke drifts up like a spirit
seeking to return home.

"Don't miss her too much
now that I'm drivin' 'gain
'cept at night
when I'm on the road
I get to thinkin' 'bout her
and I can still see that smile."

Slowly the old driver gets up
says to no one in particular
"Have a good one."

No Cedars In Lebanon

Missouri I-44 WB Mile Marker 157
Wednesday 22 July
Lebanon

Last year
cop stopped me in Lebanon
for expired tags.

this year
cop stopped me in Lebanon
for speeding
83 in a 70.

What is it about Lebanon I wonder?
Maybe there's something in the water.

Probably it's just
bored Missouri boys
from strong German stock
        and catching speeders
is their only reason for living
in the state of misery.

next year I'll avoid
driving through Lebanon.

Land of Misery

Missoui I-44 WB Mile Marker 88
Wednesday 22 July 4:00 PM
Stafford

The truckstop is still
under destruction
and the tv lounge
is on the second floor
        keeps the disabled
        and other riff-raff out
didn't see the sign saying
No Indians Allowed.

Heat and humidity are barred
from entering the driver's lounge
where the old driver wearing
a United Van Lines cap
sits in the back of the room
and watches the young couple
busy fondling each other
says in a quiet mumble
        "He's sure gonna be surprised
        when he finds out that ain't no girl."

Fried Chicken

Missouri I-44 WB Mile Marker 4
Wednesday 22 July
Joplin

I. (6:30 PM)

The smell of sweet lemon
bubbles from the pitcher
and the heat index has dropped
to a hundred and one.

Driver says he grew up on a farm
and never had fried chicken
for breakfast.

The other driver says he grew up
on a chicken ranch and had
fried chicken for breakfast
every day.

And QualComm is owned by
Schneider Trucking
           he read in Trucker's News
"Pretty soon" the waitress says
"we're all gonna to be workin'
for jes one company."
           probably end up with everyone
           eating fried chicken for breakfast.

II. (8PM)

West wind breeze
carries Cloud People
and Rain Beings
to rest at this place.

Heat and fraternal twin humidity
like the lot lizards
are banished for now.
Perhaps the Thunderbird
is no longer topless.

III. (9 PM)

In the game room
the mustached driver
concentrates on the
pinball machine
nervous fingers flick
twin paddles until
all the balls are
swallowed by the machine.
"Got any papers?" he asks
eyes never leaving the
pinball playing field.
"For smoking or driving?"
the tourist with glasses responds.
"Smokin' 'cause I already got
my C.D.L."

IV. (10 PM)

The four clocks proclaim the time
for the Pacific, Mountain,
Central and Eastern zones
and the three black drivers
are a sharp contrast
to the sea of white faces
and none are concerned
about the time in London.

The DONCO driver recites his itinerary
like a veteran travel agent
"Goin' to Cincinnati,
then Michigan,
back to California,
and then who knows where."

Bright yellow letters on the
driver's black t-shirt commands
everyone who reads to
       "Quit your sniveling"

They laugh about Viagra
which makes the waitress think
about a webpage she has
on her computer at home.

The Territory

Oklahoma I-44 WB Mile Marker 238
Thursday 23 July Noon
Tulsa

The smell of sweet sage
welcomes the People to
the heart of The Territory.

Mind-weary drivers
collapsed in the tv lounge
endure the antics of Jim Varney
in Ernest's African Adventure.

Standing at the fuel desk
the driver says he can't drop
his load til tomorrow
to no one in particular as he
hunts through the giant rack
stuffed with pamphlets.

Hot humid air mingles with sweet sage
and grand blue sky filled with Cloud People
gives quiet comfort to those travelling
through the heart of Indian Country.

16

Non-Sequiturs

Oklahoma I-35 SB Exit 137
Thursday 23 July 1:38PM
Oklahoma City

"SHOWER NUMBER THREE FOUR SEVEN
IS NOW READY" the prerecorded voice blares
and the smell of rancid grease
overwhelms the tv lounge
where drivers sit in silence
waiting their turn to take a shower.

Leading the cheer for Jerry Springer
the frazzled brunette driver
is drowned out by the silence
in response to her outburst
and only the shower control monitor
generates any interest.

And the driver in the nike golf cap
searches frantically in his bag
        the pimple on his neck
        screaming to be popped
pulls out a pack of Marlboro reds
lights the last cigarette and says
he doesn't want to have kids
because a friend of his was killed
        The other driver is convinced
        it's the fault of the government.

In the restaurant the driver says
his mom was born in Sweden where
they had day care centers that looked
like fancy banks
and the cashier says she don't pay
social security taxes
invests what she'd have to pay
for social security in
stocks, bonds, and mutual funds
and the woman driver says

her husband talked her into drivin' again
    "We fight less now that I'm
    back on the road."

Hitch-Hikers Not Allowed What?

Oklahoma I-40 WB Mile Marker 127
Thursday 23 July 2:30PM
Oklahoma City

At the entrance to the truck stop
the rules for admittance
are clearly posted:
    No Shoes
        No Shirt
            No Service
    Hitch-hikers not allowed.

        Guess that means
        it's ok to not wear
        pants or undershorts.

In this land of abundance
the twenty-something hiker
admits to not eating anything
for the last two days.

And the grandmotherly cashier
who invests her overtime pay
in the stock market tells the hiker
not to bother any of the customers.

"I'll do any kind of work for a meal."
the hiker pleads
and the cashier tells him to
go set down and
order somethin' to eat.

"It's my treat." she winks
"I have a grandson 'bout your age
and I sure wouldn't want
for him ta go hungry
when he's out on the road."

Faux Chinese French

Oklahoma I-40 EB Exit 140
Thursday 23 July 4:00 PM
Oklahoma City
Flying J

Grasshopper. Kung Fu
Magic Bowl and sesame chicken
reminds me of that restaurant in Kingman
where we ate so many years ago.

Sweat-soaked bodies
from jet-engine hot air
move in slow motion
oblivious to loudspeakers
ordering a Code 49
on Pump 21.

And the French dip wasn't
the least bit french
nor was the driver
belching after the last bite.

"You an Indian?" asks the
belching driver with the crew cut.
"Nope. I'm Pawnee," says
the man with the long straight
black-hair sitting at the counter.
"Sure wish I was Indian
so's I cud get all that free
money they do."

Pawnee man is silent then asks:
       "Wasn't it Rene Descartes
       the French philosopher,
       who said in his 6th Meditation
       that 'the act of understanding
       (*intellectio*) is distinguished from
       that of the imagination (*imaginatio*)'?"

A faint whisper
urges me to continue
the journey to the homeplace.

Righteous Massacre

Oklahoma I-40 WB Exit 140
Thusday 23 July 7:00PM
Oklahoma City

Violence and war
permeate the air
in the tv lounge
where the drivers
relive the Vietnam War
sit transfixed
as they watch Platoon
and experience the
brutality of America's GI's
        murdering an old woman
        murdering a four year old
            both shot at point blank range
      while the rest of the Heroes
      stand in silence except for
      Elias.

"What's wrong with America?"
is the topic of choice in the
Country Market restaurant
and one driver proudly proclaims
he served two tours in 'Nam
bemoans the fact that
the government didn't just go in
and kill all them gooks
right at the get go.

They celebrate violence and war
in this place where the
Murragh Horror took place
in downtown Oklahoma City
and the bomb-destroyed
vacant land is just a place
to leave flowers and other
objects of remembrance.

Corpus Christi

Two cats on vacation
in Corpus Christi, Texas
one black and the other caramel
      hang out at the swimming pool
      of the Now Open Discomfort Motel
         managed by Indians from India.

The squawking local seagull
      a dive-bomber with an attitude
      who refuses to guide the cats
      or be their meal
hovers one hundred feet above
      and lectures the cats with impunity
They lick their paws in nonchalant anticipation.

The warm insistent breeze
invades from the south and hurls
      beach sand and gulf water across
      flat scrub-tree infested land
The cats continue their vigil
      carefully stalking the swimming pool
unconcerned with the passing of time
      or the seagull.

Losing The Alamo

They say the Alamo was lost
because someone
            from Tennessee
thought it would be a good idea
            to aim the canons
            at the defenders.

They say the Alamo was lost
because someone
            messed with Texas
and Jim Bowie needed
            a shrine somewhere
            near the old Oak tree.

They say the Alamo was lost
because someone
            who was traveling
didn't go to that place
        filled with anger
            and dead dreams.

They say the Alamo was lost
because no one
                remembered
except historians
        who tell their own story
        not necessarily the truth.

Cloud People

New Mexico I-40 WB Exit 277
Friday 24 July - 2:00PM to 4:30PM
Santa Rosa

Gusting west wind
brings Cloud People
who rain down their blessing
and feed brown earth.

Thunder Beings are at play
in a magic bowling ball game
above the brown and yellow mesas
and bolts of lightening explode
like giant firecrackers on the Fourth of July
attest to another strike.

Smell of fresh mown hay
mingles with wet sheep's wool
and the cashier says
"there is no ice at the soft drink stand."

In the far distance
blue mountain hides behind
a dark jagged mountain
where a single star hovers above
to guide me to the homeplace.

Non-Vegetarian Blues

New Mexico I-40 WB Exit 194
Friday 24 July
Moriarity

The voice from the homeplace
whispers in my heart
and the old cowboy at the counter
reeks of cow manure and
cigarettes
wants his coffee black.

Says he's from down south
but he ain't no texican neither
The double negative makes me
wonder if he really is a texican.

I think of long summer days
branding cattle at the ranch
desperately wishing to be
anyplace else.

"Goin' ta market"
the cowboy volunteers
"if'n them kettle set-el din."

That's the problem with cattle.
They always know when it's
their time to be slaughtered.

"Guess I have the burr-gr."
And the whisper in my heart
grows strong.

Crossroads

New Mexico I-25 NB Exit 227A
Friday 24 July
Albuquerque

At the place where I-25 and I-40 cross
the truck stop squats like an old toad
ready to welcome the tired and hungry.

The nickle-a-song jukebox is gone
and it's a long climb to the second floor
where drivers shower and watch tv
in the make-shift driver's lounge.

"Sure was hot when I left Maryland"
the driver says to the others
straining to hear the latest episode
of the Dating Game.
"Zat so?"
"Yep. Made it here in two days."

The sound of their voices fade
as I am hurled into the vortex of sleep
and the whisper from the homeplace
at the edge of blue mountain
grows stronger.

Nine Mile Hill

New Mexico I-40 WB 153
Saturday 25 July
Albuquerque

From the top of nine mile hill
golden dots shimmer
marking the place of the
duke's city.

The brand new truck stop
is alive with travelers
eager to leave
        to get on the road
        east
        to get on the road
        west.

I remember that eagerness.

The mobile home salesman
on the radio eagerly pitches
his best deal for a mere
fifty-five thousand
and some change.

The sound from the radio
fades into the silence of
the west wind that carries
on its back the voice of
blue mountain calling me
to the homeplace.

I drown in the psychic embrace
as I raise my hand in greeting.

NYAH
SONGS

Homeplace

Sunday 26 July
Laguna

At the center of creation
I stand and bear witness
On this St. Ann's Day.

At the edge of blue mountain
I raise my hands in thanks
to the mothers
      who have cared
      for the people
      who have cared
      for me
and I sing an honor song
      to our mother
and I sing an honor song
      to our sisters
and I sing an honor song
and I sing an honor song.

Corn Mother

"Is that you?"
I ask politely.
    I thought I saw you
    buy that homeless man
    something to eat.

"Is that you?"
I ask respectfully.
    I thought I heard you
    tell the weeping child
    everything would be ok.

"Is that you?"
I ask courteously.
    I thought I felt you
    touching my left arm
    making me healthy again.

"Is that you?"
I wonder in my dream.
    Ha-aah samuti (Yes my son)
    I am the one who is here.

Nyah Agnes

Gran'ma didn't make fry bread
her Indian hands refused the mold
Instead she chose a different path
imposed her will in other ways.

White-laced lilac, cedar trees and roses
surrounded her white plaster house
Never wanted a different life
after traveling round the world.

A romantic who enjoyed poetry
her favorites were Keats and Donne
The crafted meter and tempo
reminded her of tribal drums.

She always knew she was Indian enough
took me to see the masked dances
"These are your people," she declared
"Never forget you are Oak clan."

Gave her aunt Edith "what for" over me
staying all night at the beach house
Defended my locking the door
as if she was the guilty one.

Worked every day in her private garden
dragged the hose across all the rocks
Brought precious water to the plants
Until crippled by arthritis.

Only a few were permitted to see
behind her mask of stoic reserve
Or after one margarita
or when her sister Flissie died.

Then when her youngest died of alcohol
her rock garden flowers withered
The carefully tended roses
refused to climb the white trellis.

The final stroke left her frozen in bed
and she knew that her time had come
That was the last time I saw her
surrounded by the *Kaht-sin-ah.*

"Good-bye please" she'd say
when lessons were done
her word-filled eyes still haunt my soul
"Good-bye please" I softly whispered
and watched her spirit pass over.

Gran'ma never made frybread
Now she dances among the stars
Her gossamer shawl still glitters
And at night I hear her laughter.

Nyah Ethel

Will I remember
    your soapbox and epistles
        blueberry pie and chili
        driving to California
        and early mornings on the beach.

Will I remember
    your coal-black eyes and delicate hands
        fresh baked bread and sweet juicy peaches
        Madama Butterfly and Turandot
        Sambas, fox-trots, and of course, the waltz.

Will I remember
    your stubborn determination and finagling
        occasional picnics and afternoon tea
        oak china cabinet and shattered glass
        ink stained rug and your Indian name.

Will I remember
    your Great Books and Great Ideas
        wed-NESS-day and Feb-RUE-airy
        Ceremonies of State and Inaugural Balls
        Un Bel Di and Patsy Cline.

Will I remember
    your powwow dancing and making beds
        crossword puzzles and Jeopardy
        collecting sea shells and burning sand
        cleaning beans and the morning sun.

Will I remember
    your sleepless nights and long conversations
        colorful jokes and heart-felt laughter
        blood-red roses and sea gulls swooping
        dark chocolate cake and foul tasting mangos.

Will I remember
    your love of art and beautiful music
        playing the piano and singing corridos

gasping for air and tripping on your shadow
chocolate milkshakes and M.R.I.'s.

Will I remember
        to hide my fear and bite my tongue
                be as good as and not better than
                look in the mirror and be true to myself
                cry in the dark behind closed doors.

Nyah Mary

Many-Shawls Woman
I see your vision
roam celtic fields of heather
merge quietly into your dreams.

Strong-Minded Woman
I touch your spirit
light sweet grass and candles
rest complacent behind your eyes.

Beauty-Walk Woman
I hear your breathing
float on sage smoke and water
bask triumphal in your beauty.

Bright-Minded Woman
I taste your hopes
hide among the memories
soar carefully into your heart.

Show-Me State Woman
I play your games
dance with you at the powwow
sing silently within your soul.

Kind-Hearted Woman
I smell your essence
sip roses and cinnamon
drift contented into morning.

Nyah Alene

We never danced just you and I
We often did see eye to eye
I never thought to wonder why
And thirty years have passed us by.

When we were young there was no praise
The worm has turned a well-worn phrase
I heard a lot those early days
And thirty years have passed us by.

We laughed and talked throughout the years
We hugged and kissed and shed our tears
We traveled far and shared our fears
And thirty years have passed us by.

Your hair gone white not colored blue
You lived alone your friends are few
They moved away and I have too
And thirty years have passed us by.

Grand old woman let's dance tonight
Watch the fireflies by candlelight
See the moonrise yellow and bright
For thirty years have passed us by.

Nyah Carol

I try to keep you in present time
                    message bringer woman
disconnect you from a common past
                    guitar playing poet
build boxes for all my memories

                    San Francisco nights
                              skipping down telegraph hill
                    Santa Fe evenings
                              drinking with movie stars
                    Cubero mornings
                              climbing sandstone rocks
                    Washington daylights
                              looking at monuments

I still wear the shirt you made last year
                    artist drawing mentor
greet each day with a smile
                    mother and grandmother
place memories in little boxes

                    Santa Monica
                              swimming in the ocean
                    Albuquerque
                              walking city streets
                    Sausalito
                              listening to John Handy
                    San Fidel
                              playing kick-the-can

I pass the fifty to you again
                    horse rider capricorn
spend quiet moments alone
                    entertainer teacher
add memories to little boxes

                    Corrales
                              where Lewie always played
                    Fairfax

                    talking all night long
          Las Vegas
                    hoping to change reality
          Seal Beach
                    sharing our grief and pain

I visit a thousand planets
                    counselor companion
consider well your message
                    Oak clan cousin sister
stack boxes logically in order

                    Red
                              for sun and passion
                    Blue
                              for water and rest
                    Green
                              for earth and action
                    Yellow
                              for corn and change.

Clan Mother

I walk before you
> while drum beats slowly
>> as is the way
>> as is the way

I move beside you
> close to your left side
>> as is the way
>> as is the way

I dance behind you
> keep time with drum beat
>> as is the way
>> as is the way

I reach to help you
> and hold your right hand
>> as is the way
>> as is the way

I fly above you
> in a circle wide
>> as is the way
>> as is the way

I flow beneath you
> discover *Ship-op*
>> as is the way
>> as is the way

I call your name
> tell all the people
>> as is the way
>> as is the way

I name you Mother
> *Nyah Ha-pa-ny-i*
>> *Tze-wah-t'eh*
>> *Tze-wah-t'eh*

Nyah Kay

White ivory glitters
in a bed of dark mahogany
where you sing of joy and hope
and the notes you read
link past and future
explode into bright sound
sparkle like a summer rainbow
captured in time.

Ku-yú!t^{ha} sa-mák
(sing my daughter) for the grandmother
weave your song of memories
merge with time and space
letting pain and grief
dissolve in morning sun
bloom like the winter rose
on her trellis.

Miracle worker
cante mi hija para la madre
give your gift of lyric sound
luce e vita
because *un bel di*
Nessun dorma! Keiner schlafe!
and you shall sing her song
Je vaincrai!

Nyah SueCarol

Dream filled eyes
behind a stardust curtain
quietly watch
as heart laughter escapes
into this time-place
recognize
doll-size tea cups
and imaginary plates
carefully set on
battered card table.

"Inquiring minds
want to know"
you said and at the
powwow they sang
an honor song of thanks.

Old photographs are
all that remain to remind
us of that time and the
memories we carry in
our hearts.

Nyah Briget

Desert oasis
creates safe haven
for laughter and silent musing
by weary warriors
resting from the long battle.

Pragmatic armor
provides protection from
harsh light of Nevada sun
like dark tinted glasses
that masks the true reality.

Tears of simple grief
leave Ash Wednesday smudge
on the attitude that you wear
like a chameleon
to hide your true heart
from discovery.

Daughter she called you
understood your fears
helped where she could
to mend and fix and
in her own quiet way
supported your decisions.

Nyah Lucy

Homeward bound you travel
Wrapped in flower decked manta
Carried on ancient winds
To the place of beginning.

You held my hand
so long ago
Showed me how to become
a human being
to survive
the anger
the pain
the grief
of being temporary.

Homeward bound you travel
And I chant the ancient song
Ask the four winds to be gentle
Keep you safe in my heart.

Ahshiwi Nyah

We walk the circle's edge like expert *Shala'ko* dancers
clothed in ceremonial fashion
as we split infinity with our thoughts

        smell earth
        taste water
        feel sun
        hear silence

You weave power into present tense
mumble ancient chants to unremembered gods
and bring story into permanent time

        smell sweet cedar and pinon
        taste juicy yellow corn
        touch ancient turquoise
        hear coyote wail

I watch story scatter across the time plain
fragment into eternity across time and space
and we dare to look within time's vortex

        smell gentle rain-fall
        taste golden sun
        watch moon rise
        hear coyote laugh.

Nyah Janet

We talked of journeys
sitting on the wooden bench
renewed our links
with past and future
as bright sunlight
burst through the
San Francisco fog.

We talked of the Diaspora
of the Long Walk
of important things
like making bread
and potholders
and cancer of the cervix.

We talked of laughter
holding hands carefully
Remembered our delight
with grins and smiles
as the icy breeze
scattered autumn leaves.

We talked of going home
of the Trail Where They Cried
of certain things
like living
and dying
and walking on.

Janet died of cervical cancer in 1991.

Nyah Delia

Lilacs and roses enfold
a most gentle soul
as she cares for the People
uncontrolled by time.
        And the Holy Ones
        walk in beauty
        before her.

A timeless smile escapes
from behind a mask that hides
tears of anguish for
the children of her heart.
        And the Holy Ones
        weep in beauty
        behind her.

Time stops and waits
while she gathers pinons
and weaves dreams into reality
as afternoon fades into dusk
        And the Holy Ones
        smile in beauty
        beside her.

Wailing infant remembers
she is there to comfort
and watches from the dream-time
as she dances until early dawn.
        And the Holy Ones
        dance in beauty
        above her.

Born of Bittersweet for Salt clan
she carries the hopes of the People
carefully in her heart and mind
as offering to creation beyond time.
        And the Holy Ones
        laugh in beauty
        below her.

She honors the old ways
teaches elders to be patient
indifferent to the demands
of wretched time tyrants
        And the Holy Ones
        sing in beauty
        all around her.

And the Holy Ones walk
And the Holy Ones weep
And the Holy Ones smile
And the Holy Ones dance
And the Holy Ones laugh
And the Holy Ones sing
        in beauty
        in beauty
        in beauty
        in beauty.

Nyah Magoo

Cadbury woman bubbles with delight
Her long black hair tied in a bun
Rushes to unremembered places
With quiet confidence.

Shy warrior tackles tangled problems
Her joyful laughter grabs the heart
Like a smiling jingle dress dancer
Weaving gentle magic.

Passionate advocate has no issues
Her muted voice mixes with tears
Confused by a tyrant's strange demands
Huddles behind her mask.

Headstrong ally challenges the critic
Her dark eyes flash without remorse
Posts the faults and failings on the wall
Content in victory.

Nyah Annette

She speaks
the color of the heart
as we travel through time
telling our hurts
telling our passions.

She smiles
in the early spring-time sun
as we stand silent
hearing our hearts
hearing our lives.

She watches
waves scurry to the shore
as we sit by the water
telling jokes
telling story.

Changing Songs

In the Name of the People

Greet the people carefully
and say
        who we are
        and from where we come
                with respect

and ask
        who are you
        and from where is your mother
                with respect

and say
        of the People are we
                human beings and five-fingered
        of the earth we call mother
                human beings and five-fingered
        of the sky we call father
                human beings and five-fingered
        of our clans and traditions
                human beings and five-fingered

and tell
        of sacred mountain
        of sacred hoop
        of the way
        of the People
                with respect

and greet the people
        Hay-yah hay-hay-yah
        Hay-yah hay-hay-yah
        carefully
                with respect.

Signs

It said: "caution at cross walk."
I had never seen a cross walk
although I knew about
the right to bare arms
even though I wore
long-sleeved shirts
when it was cold.

There were other signs
urging caution
like border patrol and
no smoking men
and feeding birds.

The best sign of all was the
one with a large black P
enclosed in a red circle
with a diagonal red slash.
The sign was easily understood:
No P.

I didn't see the sign that said:
Diabetic Indians Excepted.

Bully In Training

"Get out of the car"
     the one with the badge demanded.

"You're Indian" she shouted
     figured it out after seeing his braids.

"Got any liquor?" she exploded
     knew that we were all drunks.

"You made an illegal left turn"
     it was the best she could manage.

"I'm impounding your car." she announced
     told them to start walking.

"The incident will be investigated."
     said the President of the University.

Here are the findings which are abundantly clear:
     she ain't no lady, that's for sure
     just a bully-in-training.

Some Kind of New Indian

They say it's easy to be neutral
when others do the work
of being human beings.

It's easy to be neutral
when others are
homeless and hungry.

It's easy to be neutral
while the storm of conflict
swirls and rages.

It's easy to be neutral
when living in a world of
pent-up fury.

It's easy to be neutral
until fury's whirlwind
overtakes and devours you.

Guess you must be
some kind of new Indian
eager to please.

Without Honor

We cling steadfast
to vaunted myths
of our own making
and They become Other
in the landscape of
our own agenda.

Our moral authority
erodes daily as big tribes
beat up little ones in an
insane pursuit of power
and economic development.

Long ago, it is said
a leader of the People wondered
Where today are the Pequod
And on this day we can say
in Connecticut operating the
world's largest casino.

We have learned well
the ways of the Other
We wash each other's hands
with the same cloth of greed
and polish our halos with
our pendleton blankets.

We abuse parents and spouses
and our children just like the Other
who we despise perhaps because
They look like us and we look like
Them only They don't pretend to be
anything other than what They are.

Once before, in the long ago time,
we forgot the ways of the People
turned away from our teachings
and the lessons we learned
for which the People were slaughtered

and removed from their homelands.

No more do the blessings of Creator
rain down on the People
And infants wail and the old ones mourn
and the ceremonies are forgotten
and the People wither and die
for we are without honor.

Hey-ah. Hey-ah. Hey. Hey. Hey-ah.

MITT
(More Indian Than Thou)

I speak pidgen indian
and white vernacular
like my urban relatives
living in fast-food cities
where we proudly proclaim
our origins wearing
full regalia at all the
powwows and sing
around the sacred drum.

Right On and *Ts'ah T'si Ha-ah*
flows like maple syrup
from my tongue
along with nonsensical
letters and numbers like
OIE and six thirty eight
at the office where we wear
three-piece suits, white shirt
and tie and visit by the
water cooler.

We agree there's no word for
self-determination except perhaps
Indian
an oxymoron at best
like civil service or tough love.

So we celebrate being
marginal Indians and
wrap ourselves in our
pendleton-blanket attitudes.

Ain't It Awful

Raise the buckskin curtain
for the play is about to begin.

(Enter Slug from Stage Left.)

SLUG: "It's not easy being a slug"

(It wails as it moves
dramatically across the room.)

SLUG: "It's not easy being a slug
             to be the one responsible
             for finding fault
             with everyone else."

(The trail of invisible discord
is the only sign of the slug's passing.)

SLUG: "It's not easy to be the one
             who carries the burden
             of being right
             in an imperfect world."

CHORUS: "Alas, poor noble slug
             We knew you well
             and today we clarify your name:

             You are indeed a slug.

(Exit Slug stage right.)

Grapes of Wrath

(On the anniversary of the death of Cesar Chavez)

Piled high on the pentagon shaped
clear plastic platter
the sweet ripe grapes cry out
to be eaten at the
harvest celebration.

Strange to remember
it was a grape picker
who transformed a
harvest blessing
into a curse
enforced by zealous followers
after he died.

Stranger still to make grapes
the preferred weapon of choice
in the battle against hunger.

I wonder when the grapes
will respond with a
curse of their own.

Fixer-Upper

For a mere thirty thousand and change
I bought into the special fixer-upper program
available to my kind for the past 500 years.

Only problem is they do the fixin'
and I pay a regular
monthly assessment fee.

The resident expert
like a used-car salesman
assures me that the
fixer-upper program
comes with a
ten year warranty
although he quickly adds
       "Nothing in life comes
          with an absolute guarantee."

Then I wake up and
go to the sacred dances.
Join with the People
to honor Corn Mother
Soar on late summer breeze
with eagle dancers
Remember myself and
my harmonious place in creation.

I had forgotten
how important it has always been
for my kind to sicken and die
to exist only as a fond romantic memory
of a bygone age of Noble heroes and prophets.

After the dances I cancelled my participation
in their special fixer-upper program.
The lesson was worth
the thirty thousand and change.

Mickey-Coyote

He calls it mickey-coyote game playing
when he doesn't get his way.
I think he just wants me to be
his very own Indian pimp.

When gran'ma heard about him
said she wasn't surprised
  "That's how they are," she said
  "That's how they are."

I look into his sky-blue eyes and think
how easy it is to whine
like coyote in the night
and gran'ma says
  "He really isn't Indian you know."

Doxology

From across the great water
they came in the name of their God
      Praise God from whom all blessings flow.

to this place of forests
and clear running streams
      Praise God all creatures here below.

and their God told them to smite
all the People of the land
      Praise Him above ye heavenly host.

and they did as their God commanded
and thus began
the slaughter of the People
      Praise Father, Son, and Holy Ghost.

The Great White Way

First the oppressor says
    I Love Indians

Then the oppressor says
    I want to help you people

Then the oppressor says
    You have do it my way

Then the oppressor says
    You are being reprimanded

Then the oppressor says
    I want to work with you

Then the oppressor says
    These are serious allegations

Then the oppressor says
    This is not retaliation

Then the oppressor says
    Thank you for your resignation

Then the oppressor says
    There is no money

Then the oppressor says
    There are no Indians

Then the oppressor says
    I Love Indians

Decision 2000: Lament for Leonard Pelitier

Saturday morning
brings phantom thoughts of
what might have been
and grand schemes like
innocence become vapor
to be grabbed by the wind
and hurled across the universe.
        They said: Parole denied

The slaughter of the innocents
continues in retribution for
the rape committed by
unremembered assailants
in mind prisons overflowing
with crimson passion and
arrogant shadows.
        They said: Petition denied

A most just war is waged
as shadows swirl and twist
in a desperate attempt
to escape the cleansing
with water and herbs
practical weapons used
to banish brutal malevolence.
        They said: Clemency denied

How calm the surface
scant space above the
rage and chaos that
smolders and flares
like volatile magma
poised to drown the
kind heart and resolute mind.
        They said: Pardon denied

It is that unblemished time

we seek to revive like
yellow roses in first bloom
to rejuvenate unborn hopes
in vindication of our innocence.
        We say: Freedom denied

Shame

I would like father Abraham
sacrifice you on the altar
of an unseen vindictive God.
I would watch in tranquil silence
as your essence is extracted
drop by drop from your hateful heart
then drink bitterroot and cedar
and vomit you out forever.
        May your children and their children
        Live in shame for what you have done.

I would like the prophet Poh-pey
bring you before all the People
to render judgement on your soul.
I would fling you into the void
where chaos reigns undisputed
listen to you scream in terror
as the vile words you spoke
return to drown and consume you.
        May your children and their children
        Live in shame for what you have done.

On Red Wings Soaring

In the dream I wander vaguely
across red stained sand
as weeping mushroom clouds
release glowing seeds
on mushroom infested land.

In the dream I hold the basket
where the mushrooms grow
and pour drops of corn
as an offering of hope.

In the dream I see you clearly
holding the mushroom cloud
as it fades into smoke
and ancient war-chant shrieks
over mushroom blighted land.

In the dream I whisper your name
which echoes on the wind
watch you soar on red wings
and your tears like the corn
renew the barren land.

Star Mountain

At the edge of Star Mountain
    it's magic time
    on the holo deck
and the command to
run program
    is given

                Not a minute sooner
                not a minute later

The shape-shifters shimmer
    into a constucted reality
        of zeros and ones
    inside a place called
        the Diner
    where Ethel sits at the counter
            wearing turquoise earrings
            and squash blossom necklace
    reading the National Inquirer
        unlike her namesake, my mother
            whose inquiry went beyond
            national boundaries
                (Perhaps it's a message
                a sign or a test)
    neither one is impressed
        for truth be told
            the eggs don't look very Ranchero
            nor did a bull run at Manassas
                except perhaps in history books
                    where truth is rarely told
            although a lot of men died there
              and young boys pretending
                        to be men
                        did too

        truth be told
            and reality shifts before
                exchanging pleasantries to
bus stop frenzy
    complete with faceless travelers
where sour ground beef

                frys on the grill
and the reek hangs in the air
            as the old wino
                    weaves through the crowd
                        a fancy-dancer oblivious
                                to the sea of confusion that
                                    swirls and writhes
                    like a blind octopus
                        in search of food
            booze drowned eyes focus
                    on the unsuspecting objective
            approaches the suit and declares
                    with perfect enunciation
                                I wasn't always a drunk
                                back before 'Nam on the rez
The suit dissolves
                    becomes a new reality
                                of an unremembered past
                where the battle wearied
                                warrior stands defiant
        speaks in a voice that
                echos through time and space
                            "from where the sun now stands
                            I will fight no more forever."
and innocent infants
            wail in despair
                as reality shifts

to the pueblo village where the bitter wind
hurls tumbleweeds across the plaza
tripping the blind old woman
            who was treated for trachoma
                    at the Indian Health Center
                        so she wouldn't go blind
            and a little boy cries
                    ma-ma ma-ma
                    please don't let go of my hand

and the blind old woman falls

Not a minute sooner
not a minute later
everything will happen in it's time
he said

as the howling wind on the holo deck transforms into

blaring radios and televisions
        announcing the tragedy
        announcing the anguish
        announcing the details
                President Kennedy is dead
        and the world mourns
        and the world cries
                yet who will weep for Logan
                who wondered aloud - it is said -
                        where today are the Pequot?

and tumbleweed becomes barbed wire fences
that enclose places called
                Dachau
                Bergen-Belzen
                Auschwitz
                Buchenwald
        and the world mourns
        and the world cries
                too late. too late.
                Lest we forget. Lest we forget.
and the holo deck pogrom continues to run
                Dresden. Sand Creek.
                Hiroshima. Bataan.
                Nagasaki. Wounded Knee.
                Somalia. Vietnam.
                Serbia. Ireland.
please ma-ma. ma-ma please.
make it stop
        "just the facts, ma'm.
                just the facts."
                commanded the defective detective

71

Ethel said:

> "There is the world that is in the mind and soul that
> each of us carries with us at all times. It is a beauti-
> ful place where I feel the joy and gratitude for the
> sun which appears each morning...a joy of being,
> when the smell outdoors is fresh, clean, and quiver-
> ing with the expectancy of what is to come...the
> gradual warming of the earth and the smell of its
> richness and fertility. This is the world I treasure."

and in an uncertain voice
the young man sings

> "God on high... hear my prayer..."

"all gone, ma-ma. all gone."

in the quiet stillness just before dawn
he remembers those who passed over:
> Pauline. Wendell. Sidney. Uncle Johnny.
> Zahia Rose. Mary Agnes. Joseph Edward.
> Ethel. Kurt. Ook. Bobbie. Uncle Tom.
> Aunt Mary. Robert. Agnes. Florence.
> Tanta Ida. Conception. Clara. Lauro.
> Latcho. Steve. Janet. and Johnny Canz.
> Narciso. Eddie. Milo. Lewis. Aunt Jessie
> Cecil. Aunt Edith. Aunt Lottie. E. Lee
> and Sweet William
> > who blew his brains out with a gun
> and Trevor
> > who blew his brains out with
> > > cocaine

"it's just not fair" she screams

> > Not a minute sooner
> > Not a minute later
> > Everything will happen in its time

as reality mutates into
> a classroom filled with children
> bright faces smiling

72

laughing children
joyful children
innocent children
       "Good Morning Miss Dove."
                                they chant.
       "Good Morning Mr. Chips"
                                they intone.

       "Buenos Dias"
       "Ke-fec"
       "Gu-wah-tzee"
       "Guuten Tag"
       "Bon Jour"
children playing
children learning
       one times one is one
              ein. z'vie.
              clet-eh. all-bah.
              san-k. see-ce.
              siete. o-cho.
              ku-kgu'me-ush. kah'tz.

"you've got to be taught to hate and fear."

    one times two is two
         tea for two
         fairies and elves
         christmas and cotton candy
         birthday cake and ice cream
         bar-mitzvah and bat-mitzvah

"you've got to be taught from year to year."

    one times three is three
         two's company three's a crowd
         gimme that. . . it's mi-ein
         liar. liar. pants on fire
         I hate you hate you hate you

"it's got to be drummed in your dear little ear."

one times four is four
              commie. fag. dummy. cripple.
              tattle-tale. nasty bitch.
              dingbat. pervert. white trash.
              fatty. four-eyes.
              scum of the earth.

"you've got to be carefully taught."

                    Not a minute sooner
                    Not a minute later
truth be told
        (Perhaps it's a message
        a sign or a test)

COMPUTER.

END PROGRAM.

Blue Mountain Songs

Common Ground

And so it is said
in the beginning was Thought
and Thought became Word
and Word became Story.

And so it is said
the People held Story
deep within their hearts
as they traveled across the land.

And so it is said
the Tellers brought Story
to all their relations
and all of creation rejoiced.

And so it is said
when the People joined together
they began to tell Story
and found the common ground they shared.

And so it is said
to celebrate Story
the People sang and danced
and created wonderful works of art.

And so it is said
the Story was good.
And so it is said
the Story was good.

Independence Day

Hot muggy air sears lungs
and the rockets explode
into stars and stripes
as they gather
their thoughts
       their words
            their story
into sacred bundles.

She tells story
about her arm and
staying at the hospital
until 3AM.

He tells story
about being healthy
and the green lima beans
wait their turn
to be devoured.

They tell story
about space at the edge
of the common ground
where mind and family
intersect.

And so story goes.

Ohio Gozaiemas

Okinawa, Japan

ISHKAY (one)

The patient sun waited to set
While we stood in another line
Eager to begin our journey
To the land of the rising sun.

On the flight from San Francisco
We slide along a cloud highway
The Kyoto woman slaps my arm
Perhaps she is angry with me.

I wonder if the wise elder
With a law degree from Stanford
Prosecuted an attorney
Restored the sight to blind justice.

They wail ancient Ainuu songs
Dressed in traditional clothing
The two elder Ainuu mothers
Fill the room with joy and laughter.

T'DU-WEY (two)

His eyes reflect a joy-filled heart
On our journey into the past
Tells stories about his daughter
Named for his father and his wife.

In this place called Ryukyu Kingdom
A small white bird glides overhead
And Stone Mountain gives strong blessing
At the Shrine I offer my tears.

Carefully we climb ancient steps
Reconstructed after the War
Walk barefoot in lacquered palace
Pay our respects to ancient kings.
They listen with great kindness

To words that cascade from my heart
A hawk slowly circles above
Where sky touches turquoise water.

CH'M-EE-AAY (three)

"Look at all the pretty sea-shells"
My mother's spirit says to me
Together we walk on the beach
As gentle water heals my heart.

From sacred island they came forth
The homeplace of ancient spirits
Deep within the forest they dwell
Keep the People from great harm.

We offer the gift of our hearts
As we celebrate and honor
The sacred ways of the People
And Thought Woman gives her blessing.

The women dance slow measured steps
That tell of ancient courtly ways
Joy and laughter in each movement
Confuses the blind white woman.

TI'AH-NAH (four)

Hidden power is revealed
As the Master Teacher dances
Each movement a golden moment
Delights the human mind and heart.

The Master Poet and Teacher
Reads from his book of poetry
And I watch as the spirits dance
While silent tears fall from my heart.

The five of us sit at table
Translate thought into ancient words

We sing to the four directions
And honor all of creation.

The patient sun waited to set
While we stood in another line
Eager to end the journey
Return to our homeplace.

Four Birds

Four abreast they stand
like soldiers at attention
side-by-side with wings wrapped close
undeterred by warm south wind.

I remember her talking to the birds
who came to visit like the one that
visited me in the early morning fog
as we waited for the sunrise.

Like her, I held out my hand
invited my visitor to come closer
to talk about life and other
important matters like dying.

My visitor had other concerns
and after awhile walked away
toward two other birds facing west.
Like her, I didn't protest the leaving.

Tequila Prime

We sit unsure unable to connect
in front of witnesses
and pretend to watch
the TV monitor
                carefully

Between sips of warm beer
we take each other's measure
wonder with only our eyes
Are you? Are you?
                discreetly

We examine our beer steins
feign interest in anything
except each other
ready to deny, reject, scorn
                vehemently

Kilroy was here announces the sign
blindly running for Kongress
keeps our thoughts distracted
until we smile to ourselves
                hesitantly

Rooted to our barstools
firmly chained by our fear
we stretch, move in silence
and wander away in our minds
                cautiously

After witnesses disappear
and the beer is finished
we decide to end the suspense
to risk being ignored, rejected
                fearfully

Are you?
Yeah.
You?

Yeah.
Hey-yah, Hey-yah
Hey Hey Hay-yah
                quietly

Educated Warriors

for Ron Harnage

Icy wind sears lungs
in the just before rising
of morning sun
where they gather
in that place
hearts filled with
good intent
to offer prayer-songs
and ask Creator
for help.

They shiver from the
bitter cold as they
create new ceremony
bring into this reality
a vision of
harmony and balance
that transcends time and space.

In the dawn light
their faces change and become
the heroes and prophets of the past
warriors and leaders of the present
elders and medicine people of the future.

I know it is important
to remember this place
as witness to their actions
I must hold this moment
in my heart.

New Year's Resolutions

I.

Tumbleweed dreams
explode in a cascade of sparks
and sacred west wind carries
the dream-smoke of our lives
like an offering to a love god
of our own making
        take two gallons of fantasy
        a cup of bitter memories
        four tablespoons of anguish
        a dash of cold reality
        mix well and serve.

It's New Year's eve and
we don't say I love you anymore
or talk about commitment
"good night" and
"see you in the morning"
are the best we can manage
as the nightly news
reports the top stories of the year
        our daily affairs are reduced to
        a collage of bite-size images
        brought to us in living color
            drive-by shootings instead of love-ins
            broken hearts fixed with angioplasty
        and Tina asks
        "What's love got to do
            got to do
            got to do..."

It's New Year's eve
and new-age warriors count coup
with email smoke signals
that flash across the world
their virulent word-arrows
maim and murder innocent hearts
under the watchful eye

of a list-serve monitor
              gone are the green forests
              where we wandered in our dreams
              with Puff the Mighty Dragon
              Peter Pan and Tinker-bell.

II.

It's New Year's eve and
her love flows into my heart and
our separate realities are woven together
like snowflakes melting in the afternoon sun
she shimmers in the half-light
a gossamer shadow as insubstantial as our love
hands reach out to touch
through the dream-smoke
              at the edge of the universe
              we remember who we are
              and tears like molten silver
              stream from blind eyes
              and I haven't cried in years.

III.

It's New Year's eve and
last week I caught myself dying
felt old as I walked the dream-way path
wondered if it was too late to
   prepare for a new journey
   purify my heart-mind
   offer myself to the Grandmothers.

I watch dream visions crumble slowly
fade into the mist of what might have been
and I wish there had been more time to
   watch the sunrise
   walk along the seashore
   plant my prayer sticks.

Kaht-see'nah dance slowly into infinity
as the masks we wear dissolve

with the new dawn
and I am content to
dance and celebrate
all of creation.

Cubero Trading

I tell her about the store
   "All gone mama. All gone."
She reminds me from the other side
   It was temporary

Charred rock and adobe brick
are all that remain
after the flames
cavort and frolic among
ancient vigas
leaving only charcoal
at the end of the
dance of death.

Dad was the seventh owner
he always would say.
Now he lives in Las Vegas
a long way from Cubero.

Cubero, my place of childhood
filled with memories
         sweeping the floor
         every day after school
                  filling shelves with
                  canned food.

Now the old tin used for the roof
is arranged in random piles
waits silently for the junkman
to carry away somewhere else.

Not even the fire could
break into the safe
carved into the living rock
on what was the second story.

All gone, mama. All gone.

         The Cubero Trading Company store, which had been
         closed for a decade, burned to the ground in October 1998.

Governor

for my father

Proud man plays accordian
and sings corridos and other cantas
and I am the one who remembers
going fishing with him after the coronary.

From Seboyeta to the grotto they crawled
praying to the Virgin and a promise was made
and I am the one who remembers
that he wore blue for seven long years.

A newspaper article recounts his triumphs
on his event-filled journey through life
and I am the one who remembers
that I chose him to be my father.

He adores you, she said quietly to me
and in my anger knew the truth of it
and I am the one who remembers
our journeys to California and Colorado.

He wanted to take me out to lunch
like we had done throughout my life
and I am the one who remembers
and I am the one who remembers.

After the Attack

on the death of my father — 9/11/01

I eat alone now
whisper over my coffee
an incantation for protection.

I walk alone now
curse in my mind
that September morning
when you went away.

I sleep alone now
mumble in my dreams
relive the horror
in dolby surround-sound.

She said you are helping
to organize heaven
playing corridos on your accordian
telling stories I never knew.

He Ain't Heavy

for my brother

Old tin covers melted adobe
and he knows about being lucky
crying for me as he stumbles
and falls by the old baile hall.

Long centuries pass and we
grow distant with our own concerns
and he defends me she says
to all his friends at school.

Why can't we be good friends
I asked again and again
as we were busy asserting
our separate identities.

We had too many issues back then
and I could only mock and scorn
and he could only lash out in fury
and we could only join in battle.

Holiday laughter is filled with
longing for another time
in Las Vegas at Caeser's Palace
and I wonder if that's why he moved.

Now, in this mid-life we share
he tells me I am a good brother
and I weep for what might have been
before memory was wiped away.

Et Tu Puer

for my son

I.
In the palm of my hand
I cradle his head as he yawns
the way only a newborn can and
I am held captive by his smile.

I tell him
       I'm glad you're here
       I'm glad you chose me
            from the other side
       I have so much
            to learn from you
       I have so much
            to tell you about this world.

They tell me
       he doesn't understand my words
He and I smile at them
       and remain silent
He stares at me
       through glittering black pools
Quietly our heart-thoughts
       interweave in the morning sun.

II.
His face belongs to an ancient-one
       filled with wisdom of the long-ago time
       as blood of celtic and mediterranian ancestors
       intermixes with clans Oak and Gunn.
We whisper his heart-name
       the one to be kept secret from outsiders
       and his eldest auntie gives him the name
       he will be called by family and friends.
At the church he is given his public name
       the christian one on his birth certificate
       and his forhead is marked with a sign
       honoring the four sacred directions.
I ask him to tell me who he is

"I'm daddy's tiger and mamma's pumpkin
gaga's sugar plum and papa's hito
and grammy's sweetie pie."

III.
Carefully I open the box and
thousands of memories
cascade into present time
> City streets buried in a blanket of white snow
> on this cold winter morning in Albuquerque
>> "It no dad. See? No! No!" he exclaims in delight
> On the highway driving past Flagstaff mountain
> I conjugate the verb: good, better, best
>> He responds with ham, cheese, bread.
> Morning fog hugs San Francisco hills
> as we ride the trolly from Powell to the Wharf
>> "We're connected, dad" he proudly announces.
> Dark night floods our Santa Fe house
> and I am filled with dread at leaving in the morning
>> He asks me to bring him a flower and a moon-rock.
> Telling him Laguna stories before going to sleep
> He looks at me as tears flow down his cheeks
>> "But what does it mean, dad? How does it end?"
> At the beach he rages in frustration as his sand castle
> is destroyed by another child practicing to be a bully
>> "Everything here is only temporary," I tell him.
> In West Hollywood childhood trust is obliterated
> no words can comfort or restore that trust
>> "I got mugged, dad. He stole my comic books."
> Might have been in Albuquerque or maybe Fairfax
> when he decided to invest his hard won allowance
>> "I got a rock-on-a-string." he boasted

IV.
The seven foot long
gold velveteen couch
now barely contains him
as he smiles in his sleep and

I am again held captive.

I am glad he is here
Glad that he chose me to be his father
I have learned so much from him
and I have told him much about
this world.

Now he understands why
Laguna stories do not end.

.

Dream Time

Here
where past and future argue
diverse voices utter
strange incantations
within the matrix of chaos.

Here
on the plane of infinity
where snow angels wait
the data stream bubbles
like sheepcamp stew.

Here
in the center of creation
they tell story
and I watch carefully
as they become human beings.

Here
I am witness as they walk
to the beyond place
eyes fixed on the light
hold them in my heart.

Here
in the dream time
we meet and touch.

About the Poet

Lee Francis is Laguna Pueblo, Anishinabe and Scots (Gunn Clan) on his mother's side and Lebanese on his father's. He spent the first fourteen years of his life in Cubero, a small Mexican land grant town located two miles from the Laguna Pueblo reservation.

Currently, Lee is the National Director of Wordcraft Circle of Native Writers and Storytellers. The vision of this international organization of Native storytellers and writers representing over 120 sovereign Native nations from 42 states, Canada, Mexico as well as non-Native members from the U.S. and countries in Europe, is *"to ensure that the voices of Native writers and storytellers —past, present, and future—are heard throughout the world."* He is also Associate Professor of Native American Studies and teaches a variety of courses including Native American philosophy, Native American two-spirit traditions and literature, spirit of place, Native American life and thought, and Native American theatre.

His poetry has appeared in *Poet's Gallery, Emotions, The Magus Journal, Callaloo*, and others.

Francis currently lives in Albuquerque with Mary, his wife of 30 years. He is the proud father of Lee who recently received his bachelor of arts degree in theatre from the University of Missouri Columbia.